My Niece A to Z

Fill In The Blank Gift Book

Printed in USA

Published by K. Francklin

Cover Image: Produced by K. Francklin

© Copyright 2015

ISBN-13: 978-1519270436

ISBN-10: 1519270437

I Like Having You As My Niece Because…

My Niece is...

A_____

My Niece is...

B_____

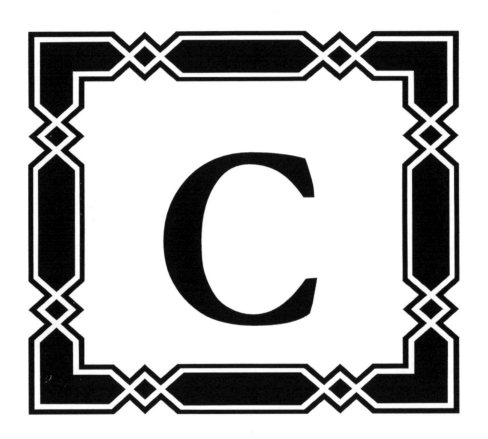

My Niece is...

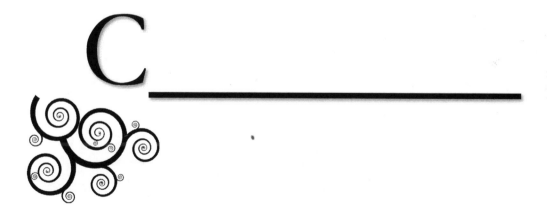

C _____

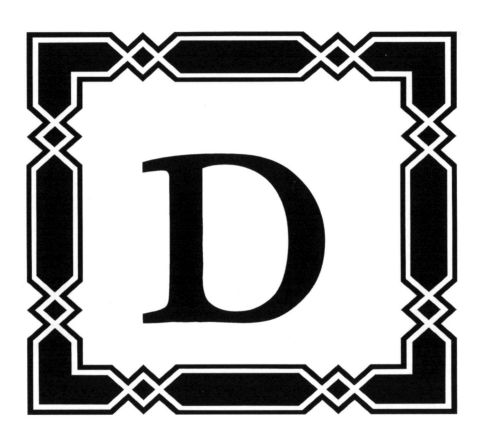

My Niece is...

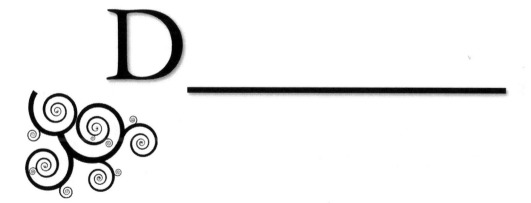

D_____

My Niece is...

E_____

My Niece is...

F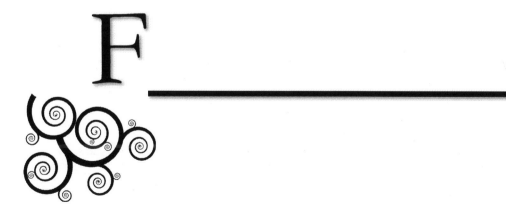_____

My Niece is...

G_____

My Niece is...

H_____

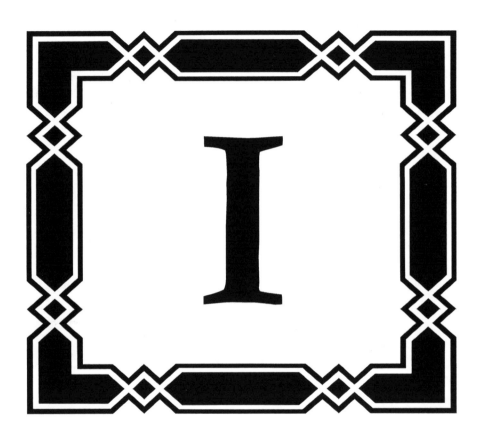

My Niece is...

I _____

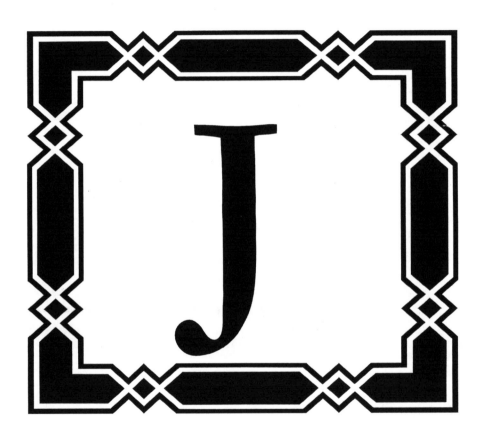

My Niece is...

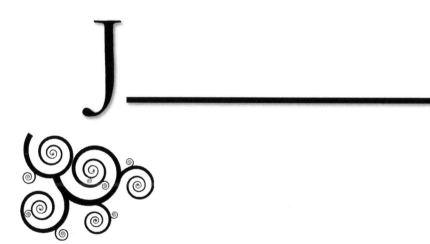

J_____

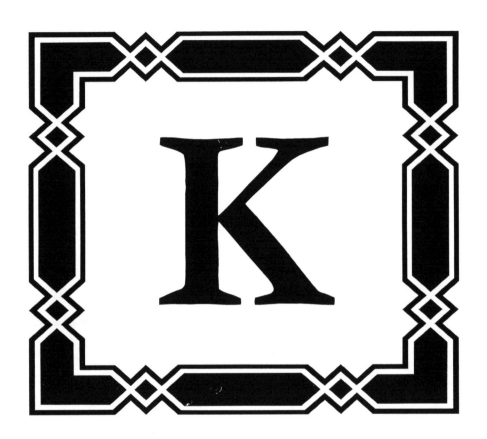

My Niece is...

K_____

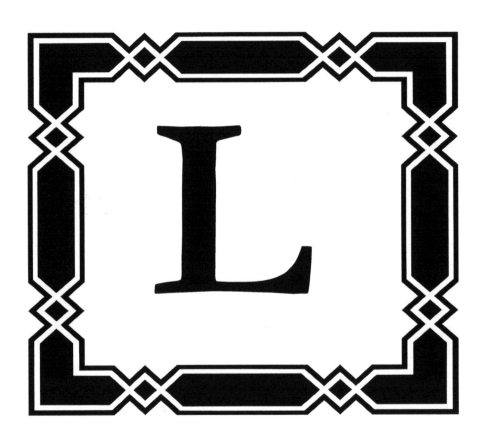

My Niece is...

L_____

My Niece is...

M_____

My Niece is...

N_____

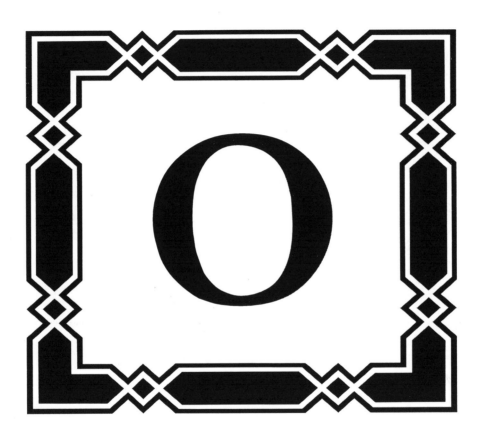

My Niece is...

O_____

My Niece is...

P_____

My Niece is...

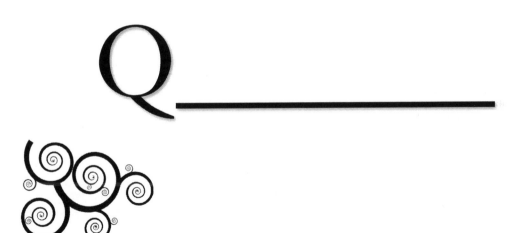

Q_____

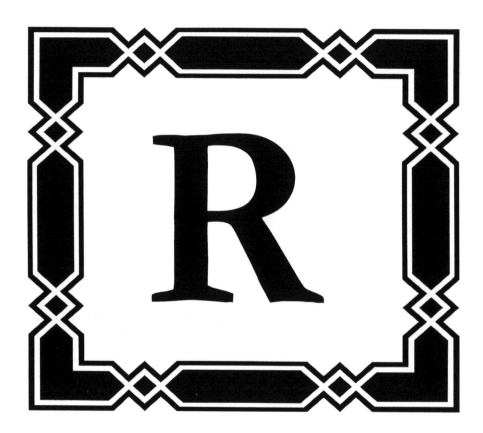

My Niece is...

R_____

My Niece is...

S_____

My Niece is...

T_____

My Niece is...

U_____

My Niece is...

V_____

My Niece is...

W_____

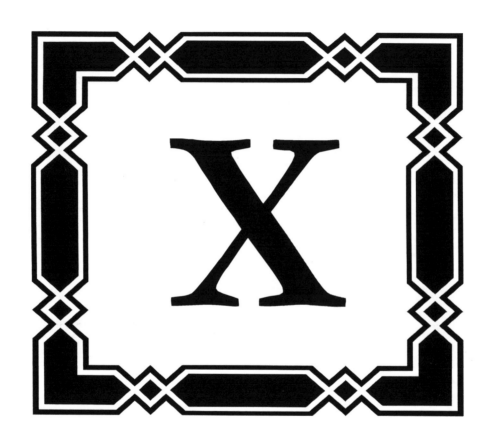

My Niece is...

X_____

My Niece is...

Y_____

My Niece is...

Z_____

Also In This Series

My Dad/Papa/Step Dad A to Z

My Mom/Mum/Mama/Step Mom/Mum A to Z

My Son/Daughter A to Z

My Husband/Wife A to Z

My Brother/Sister A to Z

My Uncle A to Z

My Aunt/Auntie/Aunty A to Z

My Grandpa/Grandad/Gramps A to Z

My Grandma/Granny/Nanny/Gran/Nana/Nan A to Z

My Best Friend/Bestie A to Z

My Girlfriend/Boyfriend A to Z

My Partner A to Z

My Cousin A to Z

My Nephew/Niece A to Z

My Teacher A to Z

96330925R00035

Made in the USA
Lexington, KY
19 August 2018